An Inspired Life

A journal for thinking,
dreaming, and discovering

Your inspired life
takes its shape from so many places—your passions
and your challenges, your goals and your setbacks,
your deepest dreams and your most profound longings.
Most of all, your life takes its shape from you. And
when you dive deep—when you begin to truly observe
yourself and the life you live—you have the chance to
shape everything your life will become.

The thoughts in this journal are ready for you to explore.
And what you discover will surprise you, excite you, open
you, challenge you, reveal you to yourself. Let yourself
be inspired by these pages—by everything you are, and
everything you're becoming.

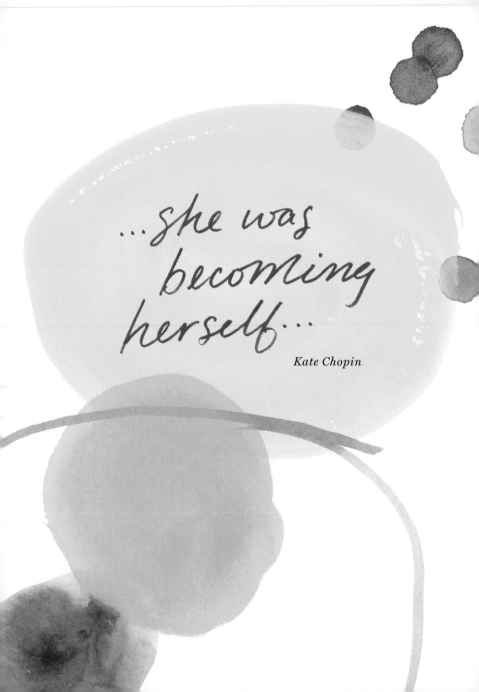

...she was
becoming
herself...

Kate Chopin

When I think about the person I am today, these are some things
I am proud of:

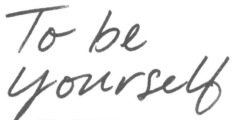

To be yourself

IN A WORLD THAT IS
CONSTANTLY TRYING TO
MAKE YOU SOMETHING
ELSE IS THE GREATEST
ACCOMPLISHMENT.

Ralph Waldo Emerson

Here are some qualities and characteristics that really, truly define me:

Can you remember

WHO YOU WERE,
BEFORE THE WORLD
TOLD YOU WHO
YOU SHOULD BE?

Danielle LaPorte

When I was very little, this is who I was:

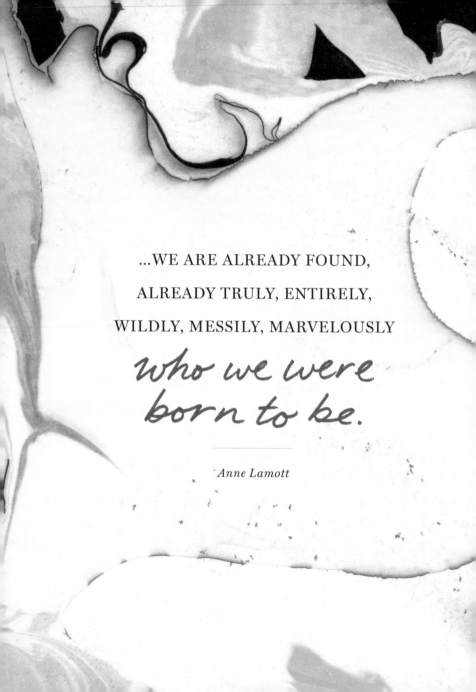

...WE ARE ALREADY FOUND,

ALREADY TRULY, ENTIRELY,

WILDLY, MESSILY, MARVELOUSLY

*who we were
born to be.*

Anne Lamott

I think these are some of the things I'm in this world to do:

THE THINGS YOU ARE

passionate

ABOUT ARE NOT RANDOM,

THEY ARE YOUR CALLING.

Fabienne Frederickson

These are some things I am deeply passionate about:

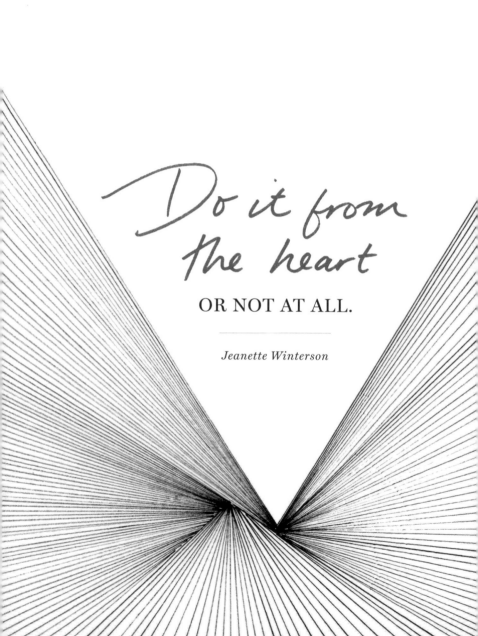

Do it from the heart

OR NOT AT ALL.

Jeanette Winterson

These are some of the things I always do from the heart:

These are some things I would like to stop doing altogether:

IN ORDER TO BE

IRREPLACEABLE

ONE MUST ALWAYS

be different.

Coco Chanel

These are some of the rare, quirky, and one-of-a-kind things about me:

Don't compromise yourself.

YOU'RE ALL YOU'VE GOT.

Janis Joplin

These are some qualities I don't ever want to lose:

...YOU CAN, YOU SHOULD,
AND IF YOU'RE BRAVE
ENOUGH TO START,

you will.

Stephen King

If my future self came to visit me today, I think she'd tell me to start:

_____

_____

_____

_____

_____

_____

_____

_____

_____

_____

_____

_____

_____

_____

_____

_____

_____

_____

_____

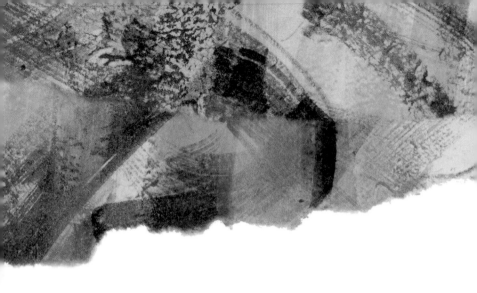

YOU HAVE A RIGHT
TO EXPERIMENT WITH
YOUR LIFE. YOU WILL
MAKE MISTAKES. AND
THEY ARE RIGHT TOO.

Anaïs Nin

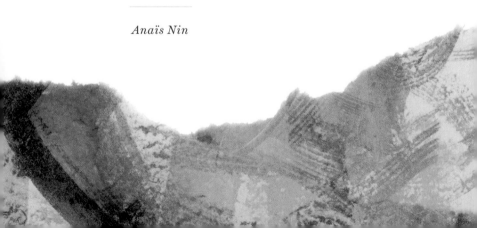

These are some of the most important mistakes I've made in my life:

Just be yourself.

LET PEOPLE SEE
THE REAL, IMPERFECT,
FLAWED, QUIRKY, WEIRD,
BEAUTIFUL, MAGICAL
PERSON THAT YOU ARE.

Mandy Hale

Here are some of the most real, imperfect, flawed, quirky,
weird, beautiful, and magical things about me:

BE YOUR OWN DEFINITION OF

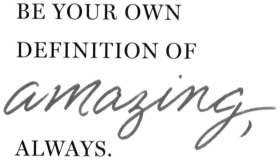

amazing,

ALWAYS.

Nikita Gill

For me, in my own life, being amazing looks like:

AND SUDDENLY YOU KNOW:

IT'S TIME TO START SOMETHING

NEW AND TRUST THE MAGIC OF

beginnings.

Meister Eckhart

I feel like I am on the verge of:

ALL I HAVE TO DO IS
SHOW UP AND ENJOY
THE MESSY, IMPERFECT,
AND BEAUTIFUL
*journey
of my life.*

Kerry Washington

Lately I am working to appreciate these parts of my journey:

HAVE NO FEAR,

*You will find
your way.*

IT'S IN YOUR BONES.

IT'S IN YOUR SOUL.

———————————

Mark Z. Danielewski

At this moment, these are some things I am seeking to make, find, and do:

IT IS ONLY WHEN YOU
RISK FAILURE THAT YOU
discover things.

Lupita Nyong'o

I am excited by these chances I am taking:

THERE'S NOTHING
WRONG WITH THINGS
taking time.

James Dyson

This is something I believe in so strongly, I'll work on it as long as I have to:

She quietly expected great things

TO HAPPEN TO HER,
AND NO DOUBT THAT'S
ONE OF THE REASONS
WHY THEY DID.

Zelda Fitzgerald

At some point in my life, I fully expect that these wonderful
things will happen:

Be sure

OF THE FOUNDATION
OF YOUR LIFE. KNOW
WHY YOU LIVE AS YOU
DO. BE READY TO GIVE
A REASON FOR IT.

Thomas Starr King

If someone were to ask me to explain what motivates me to live the
way I do, this is what I'd say:

...*find some way to break the rules...*

Nora Ephron

Here are some rules, structures, and ideas I would like to change:

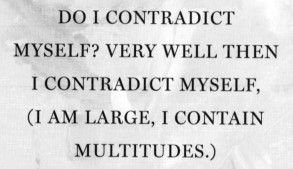

DO I CONTRADICT
MYSELF? VERY WELL THEN
I CONTRADICT MYSELF,
(I AM LARGE, I CONTAIN
MULTITUDES.)

Walt Whitman

These are some of the opposites I embody:

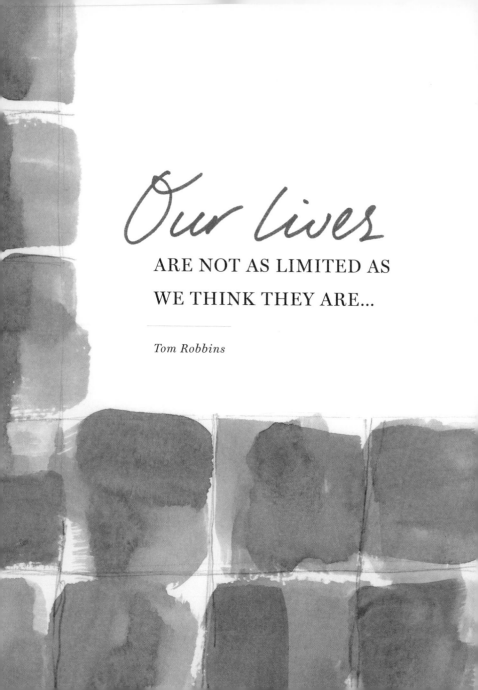

Our Lives

ARE NOT AS LIMITED AS

WE THINK THEY ARE...

Tom Robbins

These are some old patterns and behaviors I'm beginning to question:

_____

_____

_____

_____

_____

_____

_____

_____

_____

_____

_____

_____

_____

_____

_____

_____

_____

_____

_____

_____

_____

_____

IN THE LONG RUN

WE SHALL DO MORE

BY SOMETIMES

doing less.

Charles Spurgeon

These are some things I would like to find ways to do less of:

YOU HAVE MORE
freedom
THAN YOU ARE USING.

Dan Attoe

These are some small, everyday ways to make my life feel freer and more joyful:

YOU HAVE TO SPEAK YOUR

dream out loud.

Kelly Corrigan

This is the biggest hope that shapes my life right now:

SHE, WITHIN

HERSELF, FOUND

loveliness...

Langston Hughes

I love these things about myself:

YOU WILL NEVER
BE ABLE TO ESCAPE
FROM YOUR HEART.
SO IT'S BETTER TO
Listen
TO WHAT IT HAS
TO SAY.

Paulo Coelho

Whether loud and clear or quiet and tentative, these are messages my heart has been giving me:

Love
yourself
first...

Lucille Ball

Here are some ways I could love myself better:

ISN'T IT FUNNY HOW DAY
BY DAY NOTHING CHANGES,
BUT WHEN YOU LOOK BACK,
*everything
is different...*

C. S. Lewis

I can hardly believe that five years ago, I:

IN THE PROCESS
OF LETTING GO YOU
WILL LOSE MANY
THINGS FROM THE
PAST, BUT YOU WILL
find yourself.

Deepak Chopra

Here's something I worked to let go of:

_____

_____

_____

_____

_____

_____

_____

_____

_____

And here's something I gained in return:

_____

_____

_____

_____

_____

_____

_____

_____

_____

_____

THE WORLD IS ROUND,
AND THE PLACE WHICH
MAY SEEM LIKE THE
END MAY ALSO BE ONLY
the beginning.

Ivy Baker Priest

This is an ending I experienced in my life, and a new beginning that came about as a result:

...EVERY MOMENT
IS THE START OF

*the next
big thing*

IN YOUR LIFE.

Marianne Williamson

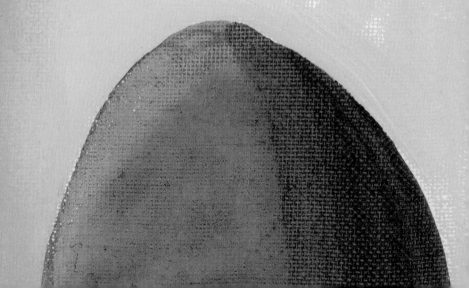

These are some new things I am open to having and experiencing:

ONLY WHEN WE ARE
BRAVE ENOUGH TO
explore
the darkness
WILL WE DISCOVER
THE INFINITE POWER
OF OUR LIGHT.

Brené Brown

These are some of the darker, more painful parts of my life that
I am working through and processing:

I AM NOT WHAT
HAPPENED TO ME;

*I am what I
choose to become.*

C. G. Jung

This is how I would describe the person I have chosen to become:

Life

DOES NOT HAVE
TO BE PERFECT TO
BE WONDERFUL.

Annette Funicello

Even through all the challenges, these are some things I have in my life right now that are simple and good:

NOTHING IS MORE POWERFUL
THAN ALLOWING YOURSELF TO
BE TRULY AFFECTED BY THINGS.
WHETHER IT'S A SONG, A STRANGER,
A MOUNTAIN, A RAINDROP, A TEA
KETTLE, AN ARTICLE, A SENTENCE,
A FOOTSTEP, FEEL IT ALL—LOOK
AROUND YOU. ALL OF THIS IS FOR
YOU. TAKE IT AND HAVE GRATITUDE.
GIVE IT AND FEEL LOVE.

Amelia Olson

These are some of the small things that inspire me most:

Dwell on the beauty of life.

Marcus Aurelius

This was one little, perfect piece of today:

THE WORLD IS FULL OF

Magic things,

PATIENTLY WAITING

FOR OUR SENSES TO

GROW SHARPER.

W. B. Yeats

This is what magic means to me:

This is a wonderful day,

I HAVE NEVER SEEN THIS

ONE BEFORE.

Maya Angelou

If I designed an ideal day for myself from start to finish,
this is what it would look like:

I AM WILLING TO BE WRONG.
I AM WILLING TO BE PASSIONATE
ABOUT SOMETHING THAT ISN'T
PERCEIVED AS COOL. I AM WILLING
TO EXPRESS A THEORY. I AM
WILLING TO ADMIT I'M AFRAID.
I AM WILLING TO CONTRADICT
SOMETHING I'VE SAID BEFORE.
I'M WILLING TO HAVE A KNEE-
JERK REACTION, EVEN A WRONG
ONE. I'M WILLING TO APOLOGIZE.
I'M PERFECTLY WILLING TO BE
PERFECTLY HUMAN.

Donald Miller

These are some perfectly human things I'd like to be willing to do:

IF IT'S BOTH TERRIFYING
AND AMAZING THEN
YOU SHOULD DEFINITELY
PURSUE IT.

Erada

Here are some things I'm afraid of, but I want to try anyway:

I haven't been everywhere, but it's on my list.

Susan Sontag

These are places I want to visit in my lifetime:

WHEREVER WE ARE, IT IS

our friends

THAT MAKE OUR WORLD.

Henry Drummond

Here are some people that make my world joyful and complete:

NOTHING IS EVER REALLY

LOST TO US AS LONG AS WE

remember it.

L. M. Montgomery

This is a memory I will always carry with me:

SING IN THE SHOWER.
DANCE TO THE RADIO.
TELL STORIES. WRITE
A POEM TO A FRIEND,
EVEN A LOUSY POEM.
DO IT AS WELL AS
YOU POSSIBLY CAN.
YOU WILL HAVE
CREATED SOMETHING.

Kurt Vonnegut

Here is a list of things—big things, small things, and in between—
that I would like to create:

If life
were a book
AND I WERE THE AUTHOR,
HOW WOULD I WANT THIS
STORY TO GO?

Amy Purdy

These are the things I want to write into my life:

WITH SPECIAL THANKS TO THE ENTIRE COMPENDIUM FAMILY.

CREDITS:
Written & Compiled by: M.H. Clark
Designed by: Justine Edge
Edited by: Amelia Riedler

PHOTOGRAPHY CREDITS: Front and back cover marble texture, pages 10, 30, 82: Pixelwise Co. / Creative Market; page 70: Pemika Chedpiroon / Creative Market; page 72: Axel Zaitsev / Creative Market; pages 78: Merrymint Designs / Creative Market; page 86: Pushish Images / Creative Market; page 94: Christian Chan / Shutterstock.